Infinite Forgiveness

How to Easily Forgive Yourself & Others

Let Go of The Past Once and For All

Infinite Power Series Book I

By Tina R. Ferguson, Ph.D.

Infinite
Forgiveness

How to Easily Forgive Yourself & Others

Let Go of the Past Once and For All

TINA R. FERGUSON, PhD

CHANCE
ALLEN

Chance Allen Publishing
Plano, Texas 75075
First Published in 2015 by Chance Allen Publishing
Copyright 2015 © Tina R. Ferguson
All Rights Reserved

ISBN 978-0-9817390-2-1
Library of Congress: 2015906857
Printed in the United States of America

All stories in this book are true. Clients have consented to share their stories, and in some instances, details have been compiled or omitted to protect the privacy and intimate nature of client breakthroughs.

DEDICATION

To the brave souls who courageously forgive and let go of
the past each and every day. May you be one of them.

CONTENTS

ACKNOWLEDGMENTS

Thank you Ellany Cevan Landry for your friendship and companionship on this journey. Thank you to my family for your willingness to share creation with me every day.

1

INTRODUCTION

I've always wanted to go see Oprah live. For years, I would fantasize about going with a friend, spending a few days in Chicago, and getting to see Ms. O in person. When she announced her retirement, I thought my fantasies would end there, but one day I received a call from a friend.

"You are never going to believe who I am going to go see!"

"Who?"

"OPRAH!!!! Can you believe it? She's coming to Houston! Do you want to go with me?"

Did I want to go with her? OF COURSE, I WANTED TO GO WITH HER!!! This opportunity was my fantasy minus the windy city!

"Yes! Yes! Yes! I want to go!"

"Great, she's going to be here with Joel Osteen, too."

Oh, my goodness…two of my favorite people in one room? Oh, my! This show would be even better than my fantasies!

The day arrived, and we filed into the Hobby Center for Performing Arts with 4,998 of our new best friends. Each of us dressed to the nines, the room's energy pulsed with aliveness and anticipation.

Soon, the subject would turn to forgiveness, though that was not what each person asked about specifically. Instead, these questions sounded like…

How do I move past the pain of my divorce?

How do I let go of my anger towards my ex-husband?

How do I …

One by one, each person asked about how to let go of an unresolved issue.

How could they let go of all that was troubling them?

The answer from Joel was to give each problem over to God. To trust God has greater things in store for you. By this point in my life, I had learned that nothing *bad* ever happens. Even the most tragic, horrible event has a gift wrapped within it that sets us off on a new course in life. I had experienced many of these types of events. I also had discovered most people never discover this deeper truth for themselves because all too often those gifts go unwrapped in favor of the person focusing on *why* the event happened in the first place.

I could feel the deep yearning within each person. Some felt almost desperate to let go of their burdens.

The hosts offered suggestions. The participants nodded indicating understanding of the wisdom shared. Underneath the energy in the room, I could feel the uneasiness within those asking for answers. Some rephrased their questions seemingly searching for greater understanding. Others smiled as if they had gained a significant insight.

If forgiving was so easy, as easy as giving our concerns over to God, then why was it so very hard to let go?

I left the show deeply concerned about this question – and those who were asking for answers.

2

WHAT IS FORGIVENESS?

For some, forgiveness is about letting someone off the hook for what they have done. When a person tries to forgive from this perspective, forgiveness can be challenging to achieve.

When you feel *wronged* by another person, the energy inside of you is active and alive. Active energy running inside of you makes your connection with that person stronger. And, that active, alive energy wants attention. It seeks expression. This energy, left unchecked, will seek out an audience. Soon, you are on the move, and that energy attracts others who share the same energy with you! You might tell your story to a friend who will listen. Others may come into your life to share their stories – similar stories to yours. It's as if magnets come together to work out like energies.

You may seek revenge. You might harbor fantasies of making the other person pay. You may even wish the other person harm. Perhaps you want an apology from the person who hurt you. Or maybe you want that person to feel the hurt and pain you feel. People who hurt often want others to hurt. The emotional energy inside of you seeks others to play out your inner drama. When you expect the person you are in conflict with to make you feel better, you will continue to link energetically to that person. And, when you continue to blame the other person, you will find it difficult to forgive and let go. Forgiveness is a *letting go* energy, not a *getting* energy.

Forgiveness is about letting go of the energy (including judgments, thoughts, stories, emotions and past conversations) you are holding against another person and the energy (including guilt, shame, anger, disappointment) you are holding against yourself. To completely forgive another person, as well as yourself, you must release the thoughts, the emotions, the concerns for revenge, the ideas about how to get even, the pain you feel from what has happened to you, and the fantasies about another person groveling for *your* forgiveness. By letting go of these energies, a new energy can take their place. A new energy offers you a chance for a fresh start; to create intentionally what you *choose* to experience.

The Infinite Forgiveness method provides a way for you to trade the energy of love for any energy that is within you that is not love. You can literally reset the energy between you and another person so you can begin again.

Reaching a true state of forgiveness is easy when you approach it energetically – outside of the story about what happened, outside of the emotions that bind you, outside of the humanness that limits you from connecting deeply with others. I'll share with you exactly how this works in another chapter.

MY PERSONAL STORY OF FORGIVENESS

I drove home with my mind full of ideas for the next work day. The pit in my stomach alerted me I was close to home – and close to an acquaintance's house. Even with my mind busy making other plans, my body knew. *Every* work day my commute took me right by the house of a woman I held in contempt. Each day, twice per day, the wrenching in my stomach told me I needed to make peace with her, but nothing I did helped. I had not completely let go of my angry feelings toward her. My inner turmoil silenced my prayers for peace. I was not yet *ready* to release my anger.

Ever since I was a little girl, I couldn't go to sleep if I felt angry with someone, or if I knew someone was angry with me. Angry, upset, disappointed – if there was any unresolved conflict – I felt uneasy and would quickly work to resolve my feelings.

I had adopted a habit of falling on my sword and taking full responsibility for whatever the issue was between me and another person. I wanted to release the unpleasant feelings and replace those with peace within myself. I didn't care what someone else thought about me as long as I felt better. I discovered others don't care about an issue if you apologize and take full responsibility for the conflict. I didn't mind taking the blame, peace in my heart was what I most wanted.

Now at 22, I faced a situation where I had held steadfast to my anger. Not for a month, or a year, but for *years* I had filled up my heart and hers with poisonous anger. I had not been able to reach the sense of peace I wanted more than anything. Instead, I held on to the injustice of the situation, and with it, my uneasiness grew. The truth was I had not been *willing* to let go. I held tight to the injustice of the situation and replayed the events in my mind repeatedly for months following our war.

The Beginning

The conflict between this woman and me started a few months before my wedding. It actually started several months before *her* wedding when I listened to stories about her bridesmaids not complying with what she had asked them to do. Frustrated by their lack of respect regarding her requests and wishes, she told me story upon story about how each had been uncaring and reckless in their actions toward her. I listened to her talk about the runaway bridesmaids for months.

When it was my turn to make wedding plans, I thought she would be a perfect person to invite to be a bridesmaid. She had recently planned a wedding. Who could be better? My fiancé had asked her husband to be his best man. Over the year since I had first met her, I had gotten to know her better as we spent more time together as couples.

During my wedding preparations, this woman did exactly to me what her bridesmaids did to her! She didn't listen. She didn't follow simple instructions. She didn't attend scheduled outings. She bought her shoes at another boutique and had them dyed elsewhere! What? The insanity!

I felt betrayed. She knew there was a logic to pre-wedding details. *She* knew what it was like to have people running off on their own. She knew *why* each of these details was important. How could she do this to me?

My anger and the frustration that followed each interaction began to take over my thoughts, my emotions – my entire life! I could barely look at her without wanting to scream and yell. *How could she do this to me?* echoed within me.

I felt *wronged* by her.

I wanted her to *pay* for what she had done.

There was *no way* I was going to take responsibility for what *she* had done *to me*.

I held on to my anger, my resentments, my fury for *years*.

Then, as God would have it.

I got a job where she worked.

I can laugh at the irony now, but that was SO not funny to me back then!

If I could have found a job *anywhere* else, I would have. But, it was a lean year. I needed a new job immediately. And, the pay for the new position was much higher than I could get elsewhere in the small city where we lived.

What could I do? I feared that she would tell everyone what had transpired between us. Worst of all was the cesspool of resentment building in my gut. It reminded me almost every day that I had not forgiven her for what I felt she had done to me, and I had not let it go either. When the new job came up, I had to face the truth – I had not let go of my resentful feelings toward her.

I faced my fears and accepted the job. My need for a paycheck overruled my need to avoid her. Yet, I dreaded the moments I might happen to come face to face with this woman. I hated the way I felt. My stomach churned. My anger blazed. The injustice! The injustice! She has wronged me!

Luckily, I didn't see her often. Working in different

departments one floor apart, when we did see each other, I noticed she didn't seem to hold the same anger towards me. When I thought about it, she had every right to be angry at me. I acted like a crazy woman during the weeks leading up to my wedding. Every detail seemed huge and my every reaction felt blown out of proportion. I didn't recognize myself. Shortly after the wedding, I discovered that I had had an adverse hormonal reaction to the birth control pills I had started taking a few months before. Even so, I knew I had acted like a lunatic – questioning everyone, micro-managing every little detail. The mere thought of my behavior made me cringe inside. She had moved on. Well, good for her!

Soon enough, life would throw me another ironic bone to gnaw on. We moved into the same neighborhood as this woman and her husband. By day, I slinked around the office building trying to avoid her so I wouldn't have to face my still active resentment and anger. By morning and night, I drove to work and then home again, and passed her house where I would revisit my wedding stories. I lived and worked on a path of my self-made hell.

One evening, exhausted by my worn-out stories with fresh feelings surfacing as I rounded the corner to our neighborhood, I said a prayer. *God, I just want to feel better. I don't want to be angry anymore. I want to be free again.*

The thought that came to me was *Send her a card and apologize for what you have done to her.*

The idea of sending her a card and apologizing sounded so much better than the hell I was living in that I kept driving. I didn't even balk at the idea of apologizing for what *I* had done. I certainly wasn't looking for anything from her, I just wanted out – out of my inner hell, out of thinking about her, out of the story that chained us together day and night. I finally had reached the point where I was ready to put the past behind me. I drove straight to a Hallmark store to buy a card. In the parking lot, I wrote and apologized for what I had done. I didn't ask for her to forgive me. I simply apologized. I told her I wanted to put the past behind us and to be friendly again – if not friends. Fueled by inspiration and the thought of releasing the plight that had dogged me almost every day for two years, I licked the envelope, put a stamp on it, and dropped it in the mailbox.

A few days later, I received a card in return. For a moment, I held my breath. *What if she didn't want to let this go? What if she didn't accept my apology?* Inside, I read only one word and one punctuation mark.

Truce!

That was it. I let out my breath with a huge sigh of relief. With that card, I put the past behind me and moved on. I could go to work and not cringe every time I saw her. I could round the corner to my house without my stomach churning into knots. I was free. Free at last!

Since that time, so many things have happened in my life to reveal the power of true forgiveness. This story illustrates only one way to forgive – one where we act out our forgiveness with others. I had worked out the issues I had directly with the person and apologized for my actions. When I was brave enough to write an apology to her, I claimed the true gift in the situation for myself. I discovered that I was most upset with how *I* had behaved. I felt ashamed of how I had acted toward her and others. I felt embarrassed about how I had made such a big deal about such insignificant concerns. Who cared where she bought her shoes? I learned that what I *most* wanted was *her* forgiveness. I didn't want an apology at all. I only thought I did. My anger toward her had masked my feelings of shame and guilt. If I could continue focusing on *her* betrayal, then I didn't have to deal with my own feelings. It was I who most needed to forgive – her and *especially* myself.

Discovering More About Forgiveness, Myself and Others

In my mid 30s I experienced another conflict that felt even more excruciating than the first did. I felt as if my heart had been ripped from my chest as a long-time dear friend abruptly quit taking my calls. No explanation. No response. Only phone calls that went unreturned. That was it. Our friendship of nearly ten years was over. Why? I had no idea.

My mind raced to every conversation in the weeks preceding the break. I tried desperately to figure out what I had done. To determine what I had done that could have been so terrible that a dear friend would not even spend a few minutes on the phone to share why she had chosen to end our friendship. She was not just any friend, either. She was the only other person I allowed in the birthing room when I had our son. *That's* how close we had been. I trusted her with my life's most intimate details.

With the woman in my wedding, my emotions were filled with anger, venom fueled by my ideas of injustice and my inner guilt and shame. This time, all I felt was sadness, abandonment, betrayal. I could not imagine what I had done that would call for such an abrupt termination of our long friendship. Emptiness filled my heart.

What did I do? Why did she do this? I asked myself questions like these over and over for *months.* I cried nearly every day grieving the death of this relationship. My misery followed me everywhere I went. I could not get my mind to quiet. I felt *worthless.* In my mind, I replayed our last few conversations repeatedly looking for an explanation – one that would never arrive.

How do you forgive and move on when the other person is not available?

How can you get closure when there's no way to connect again?

As it had happened before, when I had had my fill of misery and suffering, I prayed.

God, I don't want to wonder why. I want to forgive and move on. I want to feel better. I want to be free of thinking about this and her. I want to remember the good times. I want to be connected heart-to-heart without feeling like I am dying. I love her no matter what. I accept she had her reasons. I don't need to know what they are.

What would happen in response to this prayer would be significantly different than what had happened in response to the first one.

A simple way to reset the energy between us came to me. A simple, two- to five-minute meditation brought me immediate peace and reconnected me to the love I had for my dear friend. It quieted my questions and freed my mind.

Despite how abandoned and betrayed I had felt in the months prior to this, I was able to remember the good times – and there were *so many*.

She had been there for me when I felt I had no one to watch out for me. She was the one who taught me how to be single after my divorce. She is the one who came and helped me when my car broke down on the side of the highway – even letting my 95-lb. wet dog get into her brand new car! After her boyfriend walked out on her, I was there to encourage her to have the courage to fight for the love she had for him. He is now her husband.

Today, I love her as much as I ever did even though we have never spoken again. I have learned a lot since that time about why friendships change over time. Why people come, why people go. And, yes, as bad as that can feel at the time…there's a new beginning in every ending. Life continues to unfold!

4

WAYS PEOPLE TRY TO FORGIVE

Emotionally

People try to forgive in many ways. Some want to go talk to the person. Some write a letter like I did. Most want to come to a conclusion about what "happened." They seek an explanation. They want the other person to apologize. They want to receive or get closure before they will give their forgiveness. Sometimes this works. Maybe it will work for you. You can try it if this feels like the best way for you.

The challenge of working on forgiveness with another person is that often the other person may not want to forgive at the same time you do. Everyone is human and hurts can run deep. Perhaps they see you as part of the problem, and they want to talk about that problem, rehashing every detail. Or, maybe they don't want to take responsibility for their part of the situation. In this case, the conversation is sure to be one-sided.

Being down in the story, working out forgiveness from the "you did this/I did that" perspective can be challenging by the sheer nature of diving straight into the emotional waters that caused the upset in the first place. It *is* possible to rise above the story. Here's a quick prayer you can say when you call the person to see about talking about your situation:

Dear God, please help [Insert Name] see that I am coming here for peace and resolution. Please help [Insert Name] see the best in me and me to see the best in him/her. Thank you.

When you go to meet with the person, say another quick prayer to elevate your attention toward a higher level of understanding:

Dear God...please take our conversation to a higher level of love. Help me see with your eyes. Help me to speak with compassion and love. Guide us in a resolution that will bless both of us and enable us to be the love we are.

Emotionally working out forgiveness can feel rewarding – almost like throwing off a 100-lb. weight that is anchored in your heart! Remember to ask for the highest outcome for all involved. Let go and surrender the outcome by not asking for a *specific* outcome or result. Surrendering puts you in a stronger place of receiving love and support from God.

It's easy to try to dictate to God what we want. *Dear God, please make Susie see that she was wrong and I was right. Amen.* That might be what *you* want, but wouldn't it be fun to see what else is possible through infinite love and forgiveness? There's always a greater reward in store when we trust at the higher level of love. You never know what will happen! God gives the best surprises! They are always better than what we can imagine for ourselves!

If the person you are forgiving is not available and you want to work on forgiveness emotionally, you can drain off the emotional energy by writing your feelings, writing the person a letter and then tearing it up, through sending your feelings up through prayer, through ceremonies that allow your emotions to flow through you and out into the world where they can be released. Some say this works well for them. You can try these approaches. They may work for you.

Intellectually

Some people want to forgive by letting go in their minds. They want to make a decision to 'get over it' and move on. They talk in terms of "closing" or "ending" – a door, a chapter, an era. Unfortunately, this strategy rarely works. If only letting go were this easy! Everyone would do it!

Forgiving intellectually is challenging because the emotional energy (including the thoughts you've said to yourself, the stories you've shared with others, and the arguments you have had with the other person in your mind) stays trapped inside…in a box, on a shelf, reserved especially for the person that has not yet been released by you. The mind can't release what the heart holds onto. Very few can completely forgive from this level. Many can move on, but they carry the emotions of the past with them.

If this is your way, and you feel it works for you, then keep using it. There is no right or wrong answer in forgiveness. When a way begins to fade in its effectiveness, a new way naturally emerges. When you tire of dealing with things in a specific way, the natural progression is to move to a new way of doing things. In short, you do what you do because it is working for you on some level. When things quit working, you'll find a new way.

Putting an unresolved issue on the shelf, or compartmentalizing, *can* help you feel better in the moment. But, do not be fooled into thinking that the situation is *resolved*. It isn't. It's being held in a holding space until you are ready to deal with it. Men typically are much better at compartmentalizing their emotions and putting them aside. So are people who have been in survival mode most of their lives. We are designed to survive – we come equipped to set aside our personal feelings while we fight for safety.

A good way to see what is on your 'shelf' is to simply work with the Infinite Forgiveness Meditation and see who shows up that you've been holding within yourself. The meditation offers a simple, unemotional way to offload energies you may be carrying from your past.

Spiritually

One of the most powerful ways to let go is through surrendering to God through prayer. A sincere plea from your heart can send you a tailored answer for forgiveness that is perfect for you.

I've experienced this repeatedly throughout my life. In the two stories I shared, the answers were dramatically different because what I *asked for* was dramatically different in each instance. My life has taught me that the answer sent to us is *always* just right. *It's a perfect match* for who we are at the time when we are asking because what we ask for is a perfect reflection of who we are at that time.

In my early 20s, I was given a simple way to make peace with the situation. That is exactly what I asked for in prayer. In taking the action that came to me, I soon realized I didn't want anything from *her. I discovered the real gift of that moment* – I desperately needed to forgive *myself.* By writing my apology, I connected to the true source of freedom – forgiveness of myself.

The answer given to resolve my upset later in my life focused on letting go at a higher level – a level beyond my personality – a level where I felt deeply connected to God and everyone, everything else. I wanted to love my friend and feel her connection with me all the time – as I had in the past. I was okay with her leaving my life, I just wanted to feel her presence in my heart. *Her personality* had disconnected from my heart, but I knew somewhere in God's universe that we were still together. It was that deep, emotional yearning that brought this meditation to me. I had no idea that this would mean going *beyond my story* and connecting at the infinite level of love. I had no idea that was possible. Because I had no idea that was available, there was no way for me to ask for that. I only knew what I most wanted – to feel our connection again. God always sends the perfect answer and it is custom-made especially for you, for your heart, for your desires.

If you have a relationship with God, ask for healing around the upset you have. Listen deeply, within your heart, for the answer created exclusively for you. Prayer has worked for many. Try it. It will work for you.

When we have had enough, when we are exhausted and tired of dealing with our self-made hell, it is so much easier to surrender and ask. Until then, it can be difficult to let go of human feelings about perceived injustices and wrongs. If you are holding on to a specific idea about what you want to have happen, then praying may not work. You must let go completely and surrender the situation to God.

Here's a simple prayer that may work. Feel free to speak from your heart and allow your innermost feelings to spill out:

Dear God, I do not know what to do. I am [insert how you feel – hurting, exhausted, angry]. I know you can heal this within me. I ask you for what you believe is best for me right now. Thank you.

Not everyone can access surrender without a great deal of pain. I am not sure why we are all so stubborn about holding onto our misery, but I can assure you this is a common phenomenon! Infinite Forgiveness is available to everyone. Yes, this means you, too!

5

THE GIFT OF INFINITE FORGIVENESS

I received one of my most treasured gifts amidst one of my most heartbreaking moments. An answer to my prayers, this simple meditation was a gift given to me so I could come back to a deep, loving connection with my friend – one that was impossible physically because she would not allow it. This gift is what I want to share with you. I hope it will lighten your heart and free you from your past as it has done for me and so many others.

The Infinite Forgiveness Meditation is the most powerful tool I have been given from God/Spirit so far. I chose to give it this name because its effects *are* miraculous, infinite and immediate. This type of forgiveness goes beyond the levels of thinking and interacting physically with others. Unlike the first story, where I physically played out the forgiveness with the woman, this meditation offers you an *energetic* way to forgive that combines energies from all the other levels – psychological, emotional, spiritual, physical – and allows you to release those as you send love to the person you are forgiving. This meditation allows you to rise above the story that is playing out between you and the other person so you *can* let go, which makes forgiving easier because you are not thinking about what happened. Your focus is on coming back to love. At this level, you'll see and experience the person and yourself differently.

This forgiveness approach does not require you to be in physical proximity or contact with the person you are forgiving so it works just as well with someone you aren't speaking to or a person who has passed away. It does not require that you accept what the other person has done to you. It does not require that you have superhuman compassion like Jesus.

Perhaps best of all, it does not require you to 'think' and reason and sort through the story of what happened and why you felt that way. This simple tool discriminates against no one because it simply facilitates an energetic exchange of energy between you and the person you are forgiving.

You can use it to forgive anything – yourself, others, political parties you don't agree with, institutions that you blame for robbing you (as with the financial industry in the most recent recession), and even God. If you want to release something, try it. It may work for you.

Stories about clients who have used this simple way to forgive and move on with their lives are included in a separate chapter.

You also don't have to know how to meditate – people who have never meditated before have used this method with substantial results. There's no 'getting it right' – God is supporting you in this process, so you will *always* get precisely what you need from the experience. You don't have to believe in energetics or how this works. Your intention and allowing yourself to let go is all it takes to achieve true freedom and peace in your heart.

If you are finally ready to let go and replace your anger, resentments, shame or guilt with a higher energy – peace, love, happiness – then let's get started.

6

WHAT IS INFINITE FORGIVENESS?

To forgive on all levels, you must open your heart's capacity to let go of another person and let go of the associated hurt feelings, looping thoughts, and ideas for revenge or getting even that you have created within yourself around what has taken place between you and the other person (or group). The person who is in conflict with you must deal with themselves in a similar manner. They also must take responsibility for what they have done to you, what they have said to you, for the thoughts that they have had about you. There is nothing you can do about another person's choices. You can't force a person to take responsibility for their actions. You can't force them to apologize. If you did force an apology, likely it wouldn't be satisfying or even gratifying unless it came in the exact words *you* want to hear.

The Energetic Connection

When you connect energetically to others by wanting to gain something from them (to get an apology, acceptance, love, etc.), you feed the natural energetic connection that exists each day between you and others. Every day, we connect to others through our thoughts, emotions and interactions.

Imagine that with each thought you have, you send out a tiny energetic fishing line to whomever you are connecting with throughout the day. No matter what, if you are thinking of another person, *you are always connecting.* You send little packets of energy with every thought. If you have ever thought of someone only to have them call in a minute or so after thinking of them, you have experienced this simple, energetic connection that occurs naturally every day for all of us. Some people, especially those who are aware of their connection to others, rely on these thoughts. I know sales people that know when a client comes to mind, it behooves them to make the call *first.* Same with mothers who can sense their children are 'up to something.'

When you experience intense emotions, you send more energy between you and the other person. If you have a single thought of another person, this is like a tap on the head or heart from you to the other person and vice versa. If you are angry, there's a much stronger energy sent to the person. If you are in love, there's a much stronger connection than if you are only friendly.

Each energy has a distinct feeling, a distinct way it is "delivered" to its recipient. You might envision anger as arrows. You might see love as a rushing river. You might imagine hatred as black tar. Each time you have a thought, you are connecting to the other person with an emotional intensity based on how you *feel.*

In ongoing, unresolved conflict, you tie yourself to that person. You hold on energetically, reminding him or her that you feel wronged, and send a reminder packet of energy *each time* you think of them or argue with that person in your mind. When you consider how *many* thoughts you can have in one minute…how *much* energy one person can create and send to another, you begin to realize how *powerful* you actually are.

However, you can't escape feeling the energy you send out. What you do to that person, you also do to yourself. It's like one anger arrow for that person, one anger arrow for you, one for that person, one for you. You can't send an energy out without feeling it yourself. Unresolved conflict can *kill* as hatred and animosity drain the life and love out of *you*. I have personally witnessed people becoming sick from holding onto their grudges, their guilt, their shame and rage. You do not have to live with these. You can be free. Today!

Energetically, the same is true if you feel bad about what you have done to someone else and you are feeling guilty or ashamed about it. You are sending reminders to the person about what you have done. One for them, one for you. One for them, one for you.

Exchanging Energy With Others

You send energy (anger, resentment, sadness, etc.) through thoughts and emotions. The other person feels those energies. With each arrow you send to the person, you also send one to yourself. The same is true for others sending energy to you.

And, of course, the opposite is true. When you are deeply in love, head-over-heels with another person whether that is your loved one, your child or grandchild, your pet, your parent, the same applies. One for them, one for you. One for them, one for you.

What you can do is open your heart and let go of wanting anything from the other person. Letting go of wanting an explanation, an apology, a reason why, or any other thing that can only come from that individual releases you from your ties to another person. If you want a person's forgiveness for what you have done, this is another form of holding on. The more you continue to desire that the other person give you what you want emotionally, the more fiercely you hang on to wanting that person to have or experience what you want them to experience, the farther you are from freeing yourself. Letting go of trying to get emotional closure from someone else frees you to make a choice to let go. Surrendering all of these ideas opens your heart to the opportunity of experiencing more – *more of yourself, more of others and more of God.*

Surrender & Trust

Infinite Forgiveness begins with surrender. In surrender, you trust that when you let go of what you are holding onto there will be a much better experience that fills that space within you. In surrender, you let God handle the details as you trust all is well. You trust that the person who has been in conflict with you *will* learn the lessons he or she needs to learn *also*. And, you don't have to be the one that makes sure that they do, which frees you from being their babysitter, their judge, their jury. When you trust that choosing love and peace is the higher choice over choosing anger, hatred, revenge, guilt and shame, you can be assured there *will be* a greater gift for you! And, there *always* is a wonderful, amazing gift in store when you are willing to be courageous and let go. I will share more stories about how letting go can bring so much love into your life.

Infinite Forgiveness is not about judgment. There is no judging whether a person, including yourself, is worthy of being forgiven. There is no judgment about whether a person should be forgiven. Infinite Forgiveness focuses on releasing the thoughts, emotions and ideas for getting even that reside in you and were created *by you*. In effect, forgiveness is about taking responsibility for your *own* thoughts, emotions and actions against another, including yourself. Every person can be forgiven.

What another person has done to you is already done. It has already happened. Now, you must deal with how you feel about what happened. There is no way to feel better by holding onto the idea of another person paying for what they did and hoping to get some peace from that. Only you can resolve within yourself how *you* feel – about them, about yourself.

Infinite Forgiveness works at the highest levels of love to connect you with God and to release your emotional, mental and energetic energies that have accumulated within you and your heart over time. You receive this gift when you ask God to take these energies from you and to transmute these thoughts and feelings back into love. You *allow* this to take place inside of you rather than *making it happen*. If you try it, you'll see how the experience unfolds naturally in your heart and mind – it isn't a process you *do*.

In fact, there is no force in Infinite Forgiveness…only love.

7

INFINITE FORGIVENESS:
HOW IT WORKS

Many individuals have experienced horrible things in their lives – events so heinous they are hard to imagine, and yet these courageous souls have found a way to forgive and let go of the perpetrators of these acts. How? Because forgiveness lives in our hearts. We all can forgive. The capacity to work through and accept what has happened to you, and then to let the other person go without want or need for an exchange is what Infinite Forgiveness is all about.

But, again…

How do you forgive?

How do you let go of the feelings you have toward another person who you feel has caused you harm? Whether that is physical, emotional or psychological harm, the effect the person has had on you is REAL.

How do you let go of these memories, and all the accompanying thoughts and feelings you have toward that person?

Ask anyone who has 'forgiven' someone, and they likely will tell you how hard it was. How difficult it was to *let* go completely and not want the person to *pay* in some way *for the pain they have inflicted.* Payment can be an apology, admitting culpability – any number of things.

And, even more difficult for most is...

How do you forgive yourself when you are the one who has inflicted pain on another?

What do you do when you feel guilty and ashamed? When you feel like you are a horrible person? When you have betrayed yourself?

How does one go about forgiving God? When you feel God has allowed terrible things to happen to you, to your loved ones? Then what do you do?

When you send your anger or other emotions and thoughts out to another person – even if you never utter a word to that person, you are sending your energy to that person. At some level, the person feels what you are sending to them because, quite literally, you are sending packets of emotional energy.

Through the Infinite Forgiveness Meditation, you can take back every thought, every poison arrow, every idea for getting even, every sliver of shame, and every emotion in between that you have experienced.

You can let everything go to be replaced, or rather, transmuted into love. As you send love to the person or persons, the other energies return to you transmuted into love. Remember, one for them, one for you. When you send love, you also receive love.

Sending Energy
Every thought, every emotion instantly moves from you to the person you send it to. Each one can be felt.

Personal Responsibility & Choice

When you are willing to be responsible for the feelings you have about a situation you've experienced, and understand you can choose to let go and feel better, when you are willing to accept that a terrible thing has happened to you and it is already in the *past*, *then* you can make a powerful choice to create a *new* experience out of what has happened to you. This doesn't mean you must accept responsibility for the wrong that has occurred or make yourself 'the reason why' a bad thing has happened to you, but rather, accept that you can, as a powerful creator – working with God – choose a new experience.

Personal responsibility is a topic most people don't completely comprehend. I am only now coming to the understanding of the profound effect this idea has on every area of my life. You may think of *responsibility* as what society tells you to do – get a job, pay your bills, be nice to others, etc. *Personal responsibility* is about taking responsibility for *every. single. thing. in. your. life.* Every single moment of every single day *you, not someone else, but* YOU are making decisions about what you choose to experience.

In *every* moment, *you* choose what is happening in your world and what you believe is most important. You do this in two ways – either passively or actively. Passively you make choices by *not* making choices. If someone asks you, "What do you want for dinner?" and you say, "I don't care." Then you are making the *other person* responsible for what *you* will have for dinner by passively choosing to not make a choice. Actively, you choose by choosing to take an action or choosing not to take an action. If you choose to go to work, then you chose to go to work that day. If you chose not to exercise when you had planned to do so, then you chose the outcome that comes with not exercising. On and on it goes every single day with you choosing your experiences.

When you hold onto unpleasant feelings, you are choosing to *tolerate* the feelings of unease between you and another person. You are choosing to hold on to these feelings. You may not even have *awareness* that you are choosing it – many individuals don't realize how *long* they've been putting up with the feelings they feel each day! But, you *can* make a conscious choice when you aren't feeling well to choose to feel better. You can *choose* forgiveness and the peaceful feelings that accompany letting go of feelings of hurt, resentment, anger, guilt and shame.

When you have had enough of the misery – as my two stories have illustrated – it's naturally time for a new creation, a new energy, a new way to be!

What's more exciting is that when you are willing to take back everything you have thought about the person, everything you have said about that person, and any emotions you have sent to that person, then you can also send back to the person all the energy that person has sent to you! Taking back the energy that you have sent out to them enables you to be *fully responsible* for what you have sent out into the world. The gift of transmuting these thoughts into love is that you get to experience more of the love that created *you* and the other person does, too!

The most exciting thing about Infinite Forgiveness is that you are sending back only the energy of pure love. As you allow these energies to be transmuted into love by the Creator, by God, then there is no need for a conversation, a discussion, an argument about what happened, literally, the power resides in your heart and your willingness to rise above the situation that occurred so you can embrace a new experience in your life.

Consider that for a moment. The power is within **you** to *completely* resolve *any* emotional upset with another. Whether that is a parent, a child, a loved one, a co-worker, your boss, an ex-lover, a sibling, a perpetrator who has harmed you, God – it does not matter who it is, you have the power to take back the energy that you have sent to them and to take back the part of you that you have allowed them to reside within.

You were born to be free.

8

INFINITE FORGIVENESS: WHY IT WORKS

When you hold active emotional energy against others and yourself, you set up a guest bedroom for that energy to live within you. If you visit the energy moment to moment, mentally arguing with another person, fighting with the person emotionally, with each thought, with each jab, with each outburst, you continue to build a stronger and stronger energetic link or connection with that person. This is like running back and forth from where you are living to the guest bedroom every time you have a thought. How exhausting! Your mind isn't built for that kind of back and forth. These are the looping thought patterns that can overtake your mind.

Now imagine the more emotion you have, the stronger the link you create with the other person. Think of this connection as a phone line between you and the other person. As you send thoughts and emotion over to the person and continue playing into the story with the other person, this phone line gets bigger and bigger, thicker and thicker in circumference. Some phone lines are as thin as a fishing line, and some are as thick as a tree trunk! How would you like for your heart to have a tree trunk of muck running between you and the other person? This is akin to handcuffing yourself to the person you can't stand! You become a prisoner of your thoughts and emotions. You are keeping the energy between you and the other person alive through every single thought and feeling you have about them.

Trust comes back into the picture as you begin to understand that when you let go of holding onto the person, *you* can experience *more* – more peace, more love, more *you (the real you)* – you let the other person go, trusting that person will find their way and will learn their lessons. By letting go of your need to be judge and jury about what another person does, you trust a higher force to resolve the issues with that other person. When you do this, this person moves out of your guest room, and you can get on with your life! You've kissed that experience good-bye!

If you have ever acted like someone you are not because you have become so angry or upset, then you know what it is like to lose yourself in your emotions. Being hijacked by emotions running through you aimed at another person robs you of your life.

If you are the type of person that does not blame others, and instead blames yourself, the prison is the same. Instead of others being in the guest bedroom, you've put yourself in there. A time-out for being 'bad' is the same as blaming someone else. Both are interior prisons that take you out of your heart, away from living and away from others.

Choose to free yourself. It's just one choice away!

9

INFINITE FORGIVENESS:
AN EXPERIENCE IN ALLOWING

Prayer works amazingly well to release energies we hold inside. God can take anything from you and replace it with love and peace. But, can *you* let go so that can happen? Many of us can't. We don't know how. We don't know how to let go. That's okay. The Infinite Forgiveness Meditation sets up your connection to God and then puts you in a place of allowing. It's the next best thing to a quick prayer!

Allowing is a form of receiving. No active effort required. If you allow someone to pick up your dinner plate after dinner, you aren't trying to give them the dinner plate with your hand while they are trying to pick it up. You are simply sitting there, watching them pick up the plate, and you are *allowing* them to do it.

The Infinite Forgiveness Meditation works exactly the same way. You easily will watch and *allow* the love to move between you and the other person. You can simply watch as the exchange takes place. Exactly like letting the plate go, you'll release the less-than-love energies – whether those are bitterness, anger, resentment, irritation, sadness, grief, guilt, shame – between you and another.

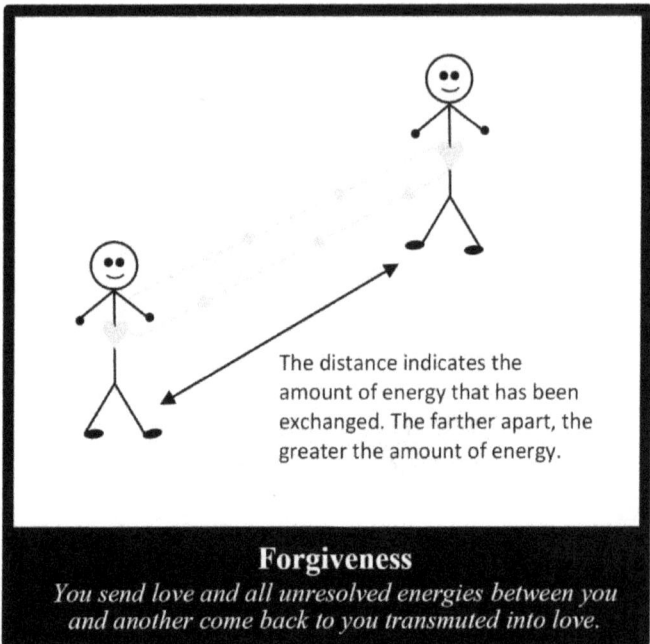

The distance indicates the amount of energy that has been exchanged. The farther apart, the greater the amount of energy.

Forgiveness

You send love and all unresolved energies between you and another come back to you transmuted into love.

During the Infinite Forgiveness process, you will be able to see the distance created between you and another person through emotional discord. By going into the meditation in a relaxed, open awareness, you will get to see and experience more than if you are trying to make things happen. Consider this is like a journey where you are watching and have a front-row seat to 'see what happens.'

The only focus is on sending love to the person or group you are forgiving. Everything else is about allowing the process to unfold. You are divinely supported in all ways, so enjoy the journey!

10

INFINITE FORGIVENESS:
THE MEDITATION

1. The meditation is simple. Lie down, relax as you would if you were lying down to take a nap. Relax every part of your body. If you already know how to meditate, simply go into a relaxed state as you would before meditating.

2. Now, imagine a pet, a place, an experience – whatever connects you to *intense* feelings of love. Whatever you choose must evoke *intense* heartfelt feelings within you. You may imagine a place you've visited where you have felt a powerful connection to the land – where you may have felt overcome with feelings of gratitude to be alive. Perhaps sitting on the beach fills you with this sensation. Maybe you remember a moment in time where you felt like you were one with everything – allow the moment to come to you. Don't try too hard to determine what is best or actively try to 'think' of an object or place. Relax and allow the perfect symbol of love *for you* to come to mind. Be patient. Listen intently. Notice what comes.

a. Pets are particularly good for bringing love into our hearts. It does not matter if they are living or if they have passed. Pets work well because there is little that is *not* love between a person and a beloved pet. Whereas working with another person as your object, there could be love, but also many other emotions linked up within the connection.

b. I do NOT recommend utilizing a living person for this process because you are working with energetics and the person may feel these energies. Choosing to work with a person's energy is like you are calling a person and connecting them into a party-line for your meditation. They may not *actively* participate, but with energy, they can still feel the effects.

c. You could also choose to work with God, Jesus or another beloved Saint. Let your feelings be your guide. Many people *love* Jesus, but the love may feel *remote* – far away, as if it can't be felt within their physical body. The sensation in the body is not enveloping because the person has not brought their love for Jesus *into* their body. Some *do* have an intense connection with Jesus, and that *can* work, too. Choose what brings intense feelings of love and joy *in* to your body.

d. I do tend to suggest animals and pets because they can be such wonderful supporters of this energetic process. Animals possess neutral energy and they are wonderful links to the earth, too. Always listen to what feels best to you. These are guidelines only. The more you work with this tool, the more you will learn what works best for you.

3. Once you connect to unconditional love and intense joy, allow those feelings to expand inside of your body and allow them to fill up your entire body. Allow that

sensation to expand so that it feels like the energy is slightly larger than your physical body is. You may begin to feel as if you are floating in a pool of joyful energy. Enjoy the feeling for as long as you like and when you are ready, direct your attention to the next step.

4.   Next, allow the image of the person being forgiven to come up in your mind's eye. Your mind's eye is the part of your imagination where you see your memories or where you remember things or where you go to imagine how an idea might work in various scenarios if you are problem-solving. When you connect to God through this meditation, you will be supported within your experience. I am not sure exactly how this support works, I only know that when you show up, so do God and the messengers. They are always with us, and by intentionally connecting in this way, you will have ample support and love in the process. Enjoy! I've heard the most amazing stories of unbelievable divine support. I believe this support is instantaneous because our hearts always retain their connection to the infinite divine and divine is always assisting us in any moment. When we enter into a meditation like this, we are *intentionally* connecting to God. As soon as you ask, everything you are asking for is given to you. You do not need to strain to visualize. Simply open your heart to allow and receive. You might see the person's face. You might see their entire body. Accept whatever image comes.

5.   Next, notice how far apart you feel you are from this person. You might get a sense in your body of across the room or down the street or perhaps as far away as another country. The distance simply illustrates how much 'not love' is in between you and this person. This

energy is the energy that will be transmuted back into love. Accept the distance for what it is – a snapshot of what you are about to let go. There's no need to judge it or have concerns about it.

6. Next, see a shell pink thread connecting you and the other person heart to heart. Allow this thread to appear…again, this is not about an active visualizing or forcing to visualize, but more of an experience you enter into by intentionally moving into this meditation step-by-step. Once you begin, this is more like watching a movie play on a screen in your mind rather than actively trying to visualize each step. Though it is hard to describe what you will experience here, my experience working with individuals is that these steps unfold quite naturally. When I would guide clients through this meditation personally, they often would see the next step before I mentioned it.

7. If you feel uncomfortable being near the other person, ask to feel better. You might say, *I feel uncomfortable, please help me feel better.* Ask for what you want. If your forgiveness surrounds someone who has harmed you, your physical body may have *real physical* reactions to the images. There is no need for you to be uncomfortable or to bear through your feelings. There is no time limit, no correct way to connect to God in this infinite place of love. If you aren't sure, ask. You will be given the answer in the way that you can receive it. Every person is different.

8. This experience may be the beginning of connecting like this or perhaps you have meditated for years. As you step into and create your experiences with divine, you will find what works better for you. Akin to learning to ride a bike, you might do what you are

guided to do at first, but then you can quickly make changes on your own. Explore. Have fun. Discovery can be the best part of forgiveness! This meditation is not about ignoring your true feelings. It is an experience above your ego and mind to commune with God and others to release emotional energy so you can completely resolve your feelings and let go. However, be sure to attend to your needs and wants as you move through it. Complete engagement enables you to be a conscious co-creator with God.

9. Now, through the thread and only with your intention, begin to send the intense feelings of love and joy to the other person. With your desire to send love, the Infinite Forgiveness begins. Once started, the feelings of love you are feeling in your body move quickly to transmute old energies.

   a. As you send the intense feelings of love and joy to the other person, that love goes forward and replaces all the other energies you have sent to the person in the form of emotional energies (anger, resentment, guilt, shame, etc.) and any thought forms you have sent (gossip, ill wishes, arguments you've had in your head with the other person).

   b. These energies instantly transmute into love with your intention to let go of the other energies and the story that is playing out between you and the person. With each transmutation, the distance between you and the other person evaporates.

   c. Through your intention to forgive, the person moves closer toward you. You will not have to visualize this movement – everything will be like the dinner plate example – you will simply witness what happens as you send love to the other person. Your focus needs to be on maintaining the intensity of the feelings of love you have in your body.

    d. Maintain your connection by staying present. Very quickly, the person will be right in front of you, face-to-face.

10. When you are nose-to-nose with the person you are forgiving, it is time to complete the meditation. You may have a thought that comes to you about how to complete the process.

    a. I suggest using the phrase, "I forgive you, I forgive myself, I love you, I love myself." When you are complete, then the person will become 'one' with you as there is only love between you two.

    b. You may see the other person step into your heart. You may see the person disappear. Everyone is different. The effect, though, is the same.

    c. When you think of the person immediately after this 'completion,' you should have zero emotional charge around thinking about the person. When you try to get back to the upset feelings, those should feel 'absent' – a void where the upset energy used to be – and in its place just a feeling of peace and being at ease with yourself and the other.

11. Take a moment to feel what you are feeling. Take the time to thank yourself for being willing to let go, and then enjoy the feeling of being complete. Thank God for the infinite support you've received. When you are ready, begin to come back to your body and slowly rise from your reclined position.

12. A short, step-by-step is provided in the back of this book.

11

WHAT TO DO IF THERE'S NO COMPLETION

If you arrive at the end of the meditation and do not complete the process in a place of 'oneness.' Trust that there is more available for you to receive in this experience. Many reasons exist as to why an incomplete process occurs, but the main reason is that there is a message waiting for *you*.

Conflict is a way for us to grow – emotionally, intellectually and spiritually. It's not fun to be in conflict, but it is part of life. If you will remember that behind every conflict is a wonderful gift waiting for you, then it will be easier to embrace conflict when it arrives on your doorstep. There's no need to fight. With this tool, you will easily be able to access the gift without playing out the drama.

If the person stops short of being face-to-face with you, ask what is happening. You will receive the answer you need based on the easiest way for you to receive it. If your intuition is visual, you might see images that tell you what is happening. If you are more auditory, you might hear what you need to know. If you are sensing, you might have a feeling about what it is. If you simply 'know' things in a flash, you might know right away what the answer is.

When there is no completion, *this has nothing to do with the other person.* The incompletion has to do with *you,* and your readiness to accept the gift and let go of what is between you and the other person.

Here are a few reasons I've seen that completion does not occur:

You may not want to let the person go completely. I've worked with individuals who have been in abusive relationships for *years.* As unlikely as it may seem that they would *not* want to easily resolve their differences and let go of the person, many of these people had very unhealthy attachments to their perpetrator. In each one, the completion stopped just short of 'oneness.' Rarely did this have anything to do with the person being *afraid* of the other person as you might suspect. More often, the person was *afraid* of stepping into their own power and giving up the story of being *powerless.* By holding onto their victim status, they did not have to become responsible for being their own person.

You want to hold on to your emotional connection. Instead of being afraid of who they will become *without* the other person, in this situation, the person wants to stay wrapped up in the drama so they don't have to become their own person or deal with the real issues at hand. If the person is busy fighting with someone else, they don't have to live their own life. I've often heard people tell me that they want *more,* but they continue to hold on to *less* because *less* is what they know. If this is your story, be brave and let go!

Energies are very active and constantly resetting. This situation occurs when the *other* person is actively filling in the gap. Let's say that you have had an argument with your best friend and both of you have gone off and started gossiping with your friends about how horrible the other is. *Both* of you are contributing to the distance between you, but when you decide to end the war, you stop contributing to the energy between you. However, it doesn't mean that stops her from talking about you. As fast as you complete this meditation and reset the energy, she can equally as quickly fill up the distance again. No worries. Simply repeat the Infinite Forgiveness Meditation.

With every reset, the energies in her will lessen and soon there's nothing left to fuel her rage. At the *most*, you might need four days or so of resetting energies (several times per day) until everything is completely neutral after a *very* active energetic exchange. Remember, as soon as you begin thinking about her again, *immediately* reset the energies. If you are watching TV and haven't thought about her in hours and all of a sudden all you can think about is the argument, you can bet she is thinking or talking about it! Simply reset again and continue to do so until all is neutral. This may sound like a tall order, but working with energy is quite easy in comparison to trying to overcome thoughts and emotions using willpower. Always remember, *you* get to choose what you want to experience.

Most routine conflicts can be resolved the first time and more active arguments may take a couple of days. Just remember, it's your *choice* how much energy you tolerate coming toward you. You don't have to accept these lower energies…you can transmute them into love!

12

TRUST GOD AND
THE PROCESS OF LETTING GO

The allowing nature of Infinite Forgiveness ensures that the meditation works perfectly for you *at all times*. God already knows what you need. The meditation is for the part of you that needs a focus while your heart and soul is *allowing* you to let go. I suggest that when you are inside of this sweet connection with God for you to keep a few things in mind:

1. **Trust what comes** – Whatever comes up, trust it.

2. **Interact within the meditation like you would any interaction** – Ask questions that you have. Ask to feel better if you don't feel well or are scared. Ask for help when you aren't sure what to do.

3. **Be open to what you are being shown or what you hear** – Sometimes you will hear or feel what the other person is feeling as you are sending love out and receiving back your old energies. Remember, the energies come back transmuted into love, but depending on how intuitive you are,

you may 'hear' or 'sense' these energies as they are transmuting. These flashes of what drives another can develop deep compassion inside of you as you relate to the other person's fears, their motivations for their actions. My experience shows me that when this happens, it can be an extraordinary gift. The dramas we play out with others are always the drama we are playing out within ourselves. The people who come to us in conflict are messengers helping us – even though it doesn't look like it. Sometimes we are so busy making others into villains we forget that they are just people with the same fears, concerns, and worries we have. Deep compassion can be cultivated during this meditation – even with the worst perpetrator.

13

INFINITE FORGIVENESS:
WHEN TO USE IT

To Alleviate Old Hurts & Wounds

Working with myself and others has shown me that every one of us walks around with a giant garbage bag of emotional energy. I haven't met one person yet that doesn't have one! The garbage bag isn't an *actual garbage bag* – it's a symbolic representation of what we each carry within our energy – inside of ourselves – in the form of old memories, open wounds, active thoughts and other unfinished business.

Consider that from the time you were born you have held every hurt, every anger, every resentment inside of you. Each of these is connected to a person you have 'unfinished' business with! How many people *are* you carrying around with you? How many people are alive and well inside of you? Does it feel crowded inside?

In my first story, the woman was alive and well inside of me, and boy was I actively dealing with her! Some individuals can plainly hear their parents' voices inside their minds telling them what to do and what not to do! These experiences are common. We all carry a village within us.

When I began working with clients for energetic healings, I repeatedly saw (within my mind's eye) God/Spirit taking out what appeared to be a giant black garbage bag of 'energy.' Some bags were small, some looked like body bags and some were larger than the person!

Spirit taught me that healing begins with releasing the old emotional residue the person holds. Depending on your life, you may have *thousands* of people you are linked up with…or maybe just a few hundred connections that are active.

Most clients I've worked with have *at least* a hundred. Don't be surprised when a lot of unknown, faceless, no-name individuals come into your mind's eye to complete their energy cycle with you! Think of this as freedom for you – and for them! It's not necessary for you to revisit every story – *thank goodness!* Through Infinite Forgiveness, God can whisk everything away and you get a fresh start!

You can take out the emotional garbage. When I share this meditation, I often suggest using it to do an overall 'spring cleaning' initially. A spring cleaning is much like an energetic reboot, and can be incredibly liberating and refreshing. This can offer you a fresh, clean, peaceful feeling inside.

Here's a list of those you may want to forgive:

- Mother or Father
- Loved One or Spouse
- Perpetrator
- Old Friends
- Past Loves, Ex-Spouses
- Former Boss, Co-worker
- Current Boss, Co-worker
- Business Associate

- Anyone You Think About Either Occasionally or Regularly
- Client
- School Bully
- Yourself
- God

When in doubt, just invite anyone you have open business with to come on in for letting go. Why work hard to figure everything out? Just ask!

To Resolve Current Conflicts

From a person who cuts you off on the highway to the co-worker who threw you under the bus in the meeting, life can be full of conflict. Some larger than others, but they all leave their mark. Use the meditation to resolve these energies and send them back to love.

Current Conflicts

- Mother or Father
- Child
- Loved One
- Boss
- Co-Worker
- Unknown Person Who You Perceive Has Done Something to You – Retail Associate, Person on the Highway That Cut You Off, etc.
- Business Associates
- Any Concern You Have and Must Address It With an Individual in Person Child's Teacher, Pastor or Priest, Accountant, Lawyer, Financial Advisor

The looping thoughts you have about what has happened to you may include replaying parts of a conversation, or saying what you wished you would have said at the moment, or just simply telling the person off in your mind. If you find your mind wandering back to the point of conflict or going forward to a future point where you show them theirs, use Infinite Forgiveness to resolve the energy between you and the person.

When you resolve energies between you and another person, you set up an opportunity for a higher level conversation or outcome. Many clients have reported near-miraculous results that they believe had to do with this energetic reset because prior to using this tool they had argued with a person for years and had believed 'the person would never change.' What actually happened is that the energy between the two individuals changed and with that shift, *both* people changed, and a new experience was then available from a higher level of love.

Keep in Mind

Current conflicts involve *active energy* that can sometimes hold *intense* emotional energy. If you use this meditation and start to feel better, and then 10 minutes later find that you are emotional again, realize that if *you* are the one holding the active emotional energy, it is *you* who is filling up the space between you and the other person again. If the person keeps coming to mind, but *you* don't feel emotional about this, then likely they are connecting to you.

Either way, return to the meditation and use it again. For the most active, emotionally volatile conflicts, you can reset energy within a few days by using this meditation each time you go back to arguing with the person within yourself. Because of its immediate and infinite effects, the longest I've ever seen for a full release following intense emotional discord is four days.

Remember, forgiveness is also about forgiving yourself. If you find that you continue to revisit a previous conflict, you may need to simply begin the meditation and ask...*Who is in need of forgiveness here?* You may be surprised that it is *your* face that appears!

In more than 10 years working with clients, I've discovered self-punishment is the greatest source of unresolved inner conflict. People tend to be much harder on themselves and are meaner to themselves than they are to others. They berate themselves, they chide, they judge, and talk so meanly to themselves. If your inner conflict is with yourself, as soon as you begin to talk harshly or berate yourself, try choosing love instead. It can transform your life!

To Resolve Misunderstandings and Rise to a Higher Level of Communication With a Loved One

We are all human. Misunderstandings stem from our inability to see another person's perspective and/or vice versa. Once conflict enters the equation, a misunderstanding can quickly escalate to full-on conflict as each person fights for the other to see his or her perspective. Before misunderstandings move to full-on conflict, use this meditation to resolve the energy between you and the other person.

If you seek greater understanding, while you are in the face-to-face place with the person within the meditation, ask to see the other person's perspective. You may hear what the other person believes. You may receive a list of fears as the reason the person is behaving a certain way. You may instantly connect to their feelings of hopelessness and unworthiness. Or you may simply know what is motivating their actions. Use this understanding to move to compassion and understanding within yourself. By going to this level, you can move out of the story you are in with them and the conflict that is being caused by misperceptions.

The way information is communicated by God is different for each person. Some people see the person talking and telling them what they wanted to know. Some people instantly 'know' what the perspective is. Some others feel what the truth is. From this place, you can then seek to move to a new perspective together by going back to the person and talking about it by first wanting to understand *their* perspective.

Some have said this meditation works like magic, and I will agree that the results *are* miraculous, but the magic comes in life when we choose to love ourselves and others!

14

INFINITE FORGIVENESS TIPS

Especially in the spring cleaning phase of using this meditation to clear out energetic connections, please keep these tips in mind.

1. **You can use this meditation for one person or a group.** This process works to forgive a person, an institution (such as Corporate America), and a group of people. You may have a boyfriend who cheated on you, and when you use this meditation, you are working directly with him and his energy one-to-one. However, you may want to work with 'all your past loves.' With this intention, you may see a line of past flames, past loves, past boyfriends. Some people report that they see a group standing in front of them, and others say they see one after another – the process is unique to you as you are allowing this divine connection. Accept the divine wisdom that comes through each experience between you, God and others.

2. **You can use this meditation to heal resentments in yourself.** Often, people hold trauma within them that

involves more than one person. Instead of a one-to-one relationship, it works more like a pattern of people that have come to help you grow and evolve. Let's say that you have felt confined by finding your place in the world. Maybe you don't feel like you 'fit' anywhere. Go into the meditation to 'release' everything and everyone connected to this pattern of 'confinement.' You don't need to know 'who' or 'what' – all will unfold naturally and easily. In a larger energetic pattern such as this, you might have your parents, a school teacher, a college professor and many other people show up to show you how this pattern has been playing out throughout your life. If you want to release *anything,* try this meditation *first*…you just never know what will be delivered by Divine!

3. **Be open to the gifts.** When you forgive each person, often you will have an understanding of why that person came into your life. The full understanding comes *after* you have released the person with love. Listen for these gifts. Do what feels best to you to thank the person or acknowledge your time with the person. Some people journal about these thoughts. Some others make art. Still others pray and thank the person for their gift. What you do with your gift is up to you.

4. **Make space for the wisdom.** After working with the meditation, if you give yourself some time to be alone, this can enable you to process the love completely. Take your time. Some people may rip through spring cleaning in a week. Some others may take months. Move at the perfect pace for you.

5. **Attend to the Physical Body.** Realizations will ripple through your mind. A shower or swim can give you

time to allow everything to flow in while you reconnect to your physical body with healing water. Listen to what your body is craving afterward. What sounds good? What do you want? Walking, cycling, running, swimming – anything rhythmic can help you physically accept the energetic shift that has already occurred within you. The release of emotional energy can affect the body dramatically depending on how much energy had been stored. Exercising is not necessary each time – be aware when you are clearing a *great deal* of energy, your physical body requires attention. Be sure to listen to what feels right to do! This may include what to eat as well. Afterward, at least for 24 hours, be sure to drink *plenty* of water. While it may seem like you didn't *do* 'anything,' you did a LOT! Remember the trash bag metaphor? If you hauled garbage to the curb, you might need many glasses of water afterward!

6. **You are the person you will forgive forever.** Forgiving the self is the most challenging from what I've personally experienced and discovered from listening to clients. Just when you think you've worked through all your inner conflicts, up from the depths of your subconscious pops another one! No worries…a few minutes and you will be feeling better again. The deeper your love for yourself grows, the greater capacity you have for accepting all of who you are – and that includes the darkness that everyone holds within themselves.

I've often heard clients exclaim, "I thought I ALREADY dealt with that!" There are many reasons why the stories we create about ourselves and others wrap around us in layers, and this topic is not the focus of this book, but do keep in mind that energy sloughs off in *layers* – in the same way we accumulate those same layers. On many occasions, this is the lament of people working through parental issues. They think they have FINALLY *completely* forgiven their parents only to wake up with more 'stuff' to release. If the relationship is *active*, there is *always* an opportunity for energy to build up between you and your parent. Use your frustration to move to love and reset the energy and seek higher understanding about how you can come together differently. If you can't or choose not to, let go gracefully! It only takes a few minutes!

7. **With practice, you can use this meditation standing up, without closing your eyes and anywhere, anytime.** If you choose to do a 'spring cleaning,' by the time you finish going through those relationships, you'll know the ins and outs of this meditation so that you can easily connect, see, and send love, and resolve the energies without going into a relaxed, meditative, prayerful state. This tool is designed for you to use on an ongoing basis that will restore well-being and a sense of peace – quickly and easily.

Use Infinite Forgiveness often, and it will get easier and easier to use! Use this tool regularly and you will begin to lose interest in your 'story' as it plays out and the drama associated with stories. You also will find that you don't care much about other people's stories, either. There's too much love to experience. Too much fun to have! Sooner than later, it will be *extremely* easy for you to hand everything over to God for release! I use both depending on where *I* am in the story. If I am down in the story with another person, I use this meditation. If not, then I happily embrace Infinite Forgiveness through prayer. Find what works for you! There are no rules!

8. **Expect people to reach out when they feel you.** When you are connecting deeply with people from your

past and sending them love, don't be surprised if they call, email or reach out via social media. Your energetic connection with others is *real,* and they *do* feel when you are 'complete' in your connection with them. This frequently happens! If the person calls and you get a pit in the middle of your stomach, be assured that this is in perfect alignment...this pit is telling you to move back to love again – there are energies that remain unresolved between you. It's up to you what action you take when others reach out to you. Do what is best for you and what feels right to you in your body. Trust your body's wisdom. It knows!

9. **Enjoy your experience.** This tool is a super highway to God and connection with others. Enjoy your time with yourself, others and God. If you aren't enjoying the process, ask for help or comfort.

I've only worked with a few people who had a difficult time connecting to feelings of love. These people tended to be cynical and harsh and untrusting of others. They had felt hurt from the time they were children and never felt love – *ever.* I often saw their hearts like hard little nuts that didn't want to open – some were like a walnut, some like an acorn.

If your heart is a hard nut to crack, invite God in! You don't have to suffer. You were born to be loved! But, you must be willing to trust love enough to invite it in. Once that hard shell is cracked a bit, get ready! The best is yet to come. Be courageous and brave and trust you *can* have and be *more.* No matter what your past experiences, you *can* have a life you dream of. Being in the middle of love and the feeling of loving energy will be a judgment-free zone, so enjoy the feeling of being loved and supported by the Creator!

10. **Once may not be enough.** When energy actively plays

out between people, such as in a conflict, you may be adding to the energy little by little throughout the day. A thought here, a thought there. One for them, one for you. *Plus, the other person may also be adding to the energy as that person thinks about you and the conflict.* For this reason, you may feel fine one day and then wake up again feeling the associated energy you once did. No worries. Simply go back to love again! Once you get the hang of this, it takes less than five minutes and can transform how you feel instantly. There's no need to investigate – quickly reset and begin again! If there's any information you need to know, it will arrive *within* your connection with God.

11. **Always seek help when you need it.** This meditation is only one of many tools given to me while working with God/Spirit. While it *is* powerful, please know that there are helpful people in this world that are here to help others *for a reason.* If you are depressed or suicidal, please seek help. If you are in physical harm or danger, please seek help. The physical world comes with its rules – use physical channels of help when needed!

15

INFINITE FORGIVENESS:
THE STORIES

Transmuting Fear and Rage Into Love

"This woman is *crazy*," a man I'll call Evan said as he started to spew the details about how his ex-girlfriend was threatening to start a rumor about him in their small town community. "My friend told me to call you because he said you would know what to do, but unless you can lock her up in an asylum, I doubt you can help me."

This well-known pillar of the community operated a prominent national youth organization. Evan had recently broken up with his girlfriend, and she was threatening to start a rumor that would destroy his reputation and make it nearly impossible for him to continue his youth outreach.

I listened to him and intuitively felt that what his ex-girlfriend was most concerned about was that he didn't care about her anymore. She wasn't angry that they were breaking up; she was being driven crazy by the idea that he didn't care about her.

I asked Evan if I taught him a meditation if he would be willing to use it until the emotions resolved between the two of them. He didn't understand the concepts behind the idea of using love to reset energy, but was willing to try 'anything' because he feared that she might go *Fatal Attraction* on him – or worse.

Evan and I walked through the meditation steps – in the same way they have been presented in this book for you. His 'garbage bag' included his fears that he would never be worthy of love, which also matched this woman's fears. He left our phone call promising to use the meditation each time he reconnected to her in his thoughts.

The next day he called.

"You will never believe what happened!" he said equally as breathlessly as he had the day before. "I did the meditation just like you taught me to do, and she called and said she wasn't going to start a rumor and that she is deeply in love with me and wants to help me with my outreach! Now I need to know what to do because she is so in love with me she wants to help me even though we aren't dating! I want her to *go away!* How can we get her to do that?"

We laughed at the turn of events, and I shared a prayer for him to pray for her to find her way. Like before, she called Evan within hours and told him she understood that it wasn't necessary that they remain in each other's lives. She shared that she would always love him and thanked him for loving her. She had never felt so loved.

It's hard to explain how this meditation works so quickly or so incredibly powerfully. Though I have been taught by God/Spirit how it works – this meditation literally erases the old 'story' between you and another, and replaces the 'story' and associated emotions with pure, unconditional love – I am still fascinated by how well and how fast it works – if only we will remember to choose love.

Transmuting Old Shame Into New Energy

"I don't know what's wrong with me, I can't seem to get

myself to move," she said.

"When did this begin?"

"About a year ago, but I don't remember the specifics about how it began."

"What is the most predominant thought you have day-to-day?"

"What do you mean?"

"I mean, what is the thought in the back of your head day-to-day – beyond your usual activities – what do you mostly think about?" With some encouragement, this client I'll call Lila was able to determine what filled the silence spaces in her mind.

"I think of my mother and she is constantly saying, 'You should be ashamed of yourself.'"

Okay, let's let your mother and your shame go.

Lila and I worked through the Infinite Forgiveness Meditation, and her mother's admonishments evaporated within minutes of completing it.

"Wow, I can't believe how easy that was! I have felt guilty and bad for *everything*. I never knew why. I mean, even if someone *else* does something to me, *I* am the one to apologize!"

I shared with her that our parental energetic connections run deeply, and they are nearly impossible to disconnect completely. When we have a parent who has shame or guilt themselves, this can easily be passed on to the child. As we grow older, though, we can choose not to keep these feelings and judgments. Through this meditation, Lila easily let her mother go so she could live her own life.

After releasing her mother, Lila made two bold decisions for her life and started easily moving again in the world.

Loving The Self and Moving Back Into Power

A former coaching client I'll call John called one day to ask about how to let go of his nagging feeling that he wasn't quite good enough. Though he had the trappings of success, inside John said he didn't *feel* successful. He felt there never seemed to be *enough* – *enough* money, *enough* prestige, *enough* promotions, *enough* praise to fill the big hole inside of himself.

After talking for a bit about what was bugging him, I could sense that he had two parts of himself actively creating at the same time. The self that showed up every day was at the mercy of the other part of himself that was always trying to 'make up' for his perceived deficiency.

We walked through the Infinite Forgiveness Meditation where he saw himself as a little boy. This little boy appeared to be himself around the ages of 8 or 9. This child didn't want to work. This child wanted to play and goof off and be silly. This child was the part of him that was *not* industrious and did *not* care at all about success.

This child had been labeled bad and lazy by John's hard-working father. John had carried on his father's torch judging this carefree, jovial part of himself that enjoyed having a good time.

As John began sending love to this child within – he quickly discovered that this was a *very important* part of himself. Minute by minute, he began to feel lighter. I could feel his entire energy change and shift with the acceptance of this part of himself that was frivolous and carefree.

It turned out that John was driving himself crazy trying to prove he was *not* that kid. Almost like trying to run away with a giant monkey on his back, he wanted to prove to the world he *wasn't* the part of himself he knew he really was inside. He wanted to show all of his accolades, his awards, his financial status to *prove* he was not *that* lazy kid.

The nagging feelings subsided, and John became even *more* successful financially as he lightened up and became more relaxed at work. He started spending more time *playing* both personally and professionally. His accomplishments grew as he worked less and relaxed more into the person he knew he was inside – a person who enjoys working *while* having a good time. He called to laugh about how he wished he would have known *years earlier* to hang out with this 'little guy' inside!

Moving From Fearful to Fearless and an Intentional Creator

Going through a divorce is never easy, but going through a divorce with an abusive, volatile spouse is even more harrowing.

A client I'll call Kristen called to ask about what to do with her ex-husband. According to Kristen, her husband had been physically and emotionally abusive for most of their six-year relationship. Though he had never laid hands on their children, he was threatening to take them and flee the city. He was wild with anger and furious that she was dating again.

He wanted her to *pay* for how he was feeling inside.

As hard as it is to face someone who has hurt you, it can be done. This meditation links you energetically to the person, so the feelings you feel within this process are real. Kristen started to hyperventilate in reaction to being in proximity with her soon-to-be ex-husband even though she was doing it only in her mind's eye or imagination.

He moved somewhat close to her pretty quickly, but when the two were about a foot apart, no matter how much love she sent to him, he wouldn't budge. We asked for help and what she received was that this man was giving her a gift, but she was refusing to accept the gift.

He was giving her the gift of *voice*. It was now her turn to speak. To speak out. To use her *voice*. But, she had not done it in either of her previous marriages. Now in the final days of this marriage, this man was acting like a wild person, linking up to her energetically to help her *find her voice*.

Kristen appeared to instantly understand what that meant. She said she refused to make any decisions in the divorce or the custody hearing. She had not spoken up when she wanted to because she was afraid.

Within her connection to God, she gained reassurance that her soon-to-be-ex would not harm her or her children. She left the phone call knowing it was time for her to make decisions, to use her voice, and to begin to speak up for herself and her children.

I suggested that Kristen take action on what she most wanted to create between them – a smooth outcome for the divorce and a supervised visitation schedule. Only she could put these outcomes into action. And, she did. She also worked within the system, with many people within the court system to ensure she and her children were protected.

I also suggested that once she took action, that she work with the Infinite Forgiveness Meditation again, and resolve all energies between her and her ex. I shared that she may need to do it often due to the active emotional energy moving between them through the hearings. When she could think of him and have no physical response and no emotional thought other than a neutral feeling – the same feeling a person might have with an acquaintance – not good nor bad, just neutral, she would know all was complete between them.

Within a couple of months, everything resolved. Her ex-husband got a new girlfriend to focus his attention on, and Kristen continued to date the man who is now her husband.

Forgotten and Forgiven For Good

"No one ever gets over a violation like I've been through."

I listened intently as a woman I'll call Zoe shared her deepest pain.

"It's not fair that these violators get to inflict their pain on us and we are stuck with them forever."

Rape leaves its mark on every person who has experienced its clutches. Her rape had taken place nearly 25 years earlier, and today it was as fresh as if it happened the week before.

"What did the rape give to you? Beyond this pain, what did the rape teach you about yourself?" I asked.

Silence filled the space between us. I could feel her grappling for an answer.

"I can't think of one thing," she said.

"What has the rape robbed you of?"

"It has taken away my courage. I used to be a carefree, courageous girl who loved the world and went out into it with gusto! I hate the man that took that from me! I HATE him!"

"What would happen if you traded your hatred toward him for your courage? Would you be willing to trade those?"

"You mean am I willing to let him off the hook for what he did to me? Absolutely NOT!"

"I can see why you feel the way you do, but when you insist on holding him by the throat, you do the same to yourself. You cut yourself off at the throat, too."

Zoe had started working with me because she didn't know what to do in her business. She found herself at a crossroad – go forward with the venture she was in, or start over with something new. She was at a crossroad with her rapist, too – the perpetrator who had stolen her courageous voice. She held him by the throat and in doing so, held herself at the throat, too. Would she allow him to keep her prisoner or would she release him and herself at the same time?

"Why didn't you do anything at the time of your rape to bring this man to justice?" I asked.

"What? What do you mean?"

"Why didn't you try to find him? Did you go looking for

him so he could be taken to jail?"

"I, I didn't think that anyone would listen. I didn't think it would matter. Who was I to..." her voice trailed off.

"Do you think it is time to let this go? To realize that you had a time when you could have fought for justice, but you chose not to?"

"I, I guess so," the somberness in her voice told the tale. It's easy to blame others instead of yourself. It's easy to say someone *else* did this to me, but to admit when you've not stood up for *yourself*...well, that is another story.

The truth does not kill us, but it does make us *feel.* Truth connects us deeply to our hearts and to what we know is true for ourselves and others.

"It's okay that you were not courageous in that moment. It's okay that you did not fight. How did that help you get what you most wanted at the time?"

She thought about it and the answer came bubbling forth. "That rape tamed me. Before, I was a wild stallion, galloping and gallivanting around the world. I wanted to explore and experience everything! This was in direct opposition to wanting to be married and to start a family. The rape snuffed out my courage, my zest for exploration and I soon was engaged, married and had a child."

"Do you believe it is time to let go of this rapist? To see this event helped you make a decision you weren't willing to make consciously for yourself? To accept the gift of *that* moment was wrapped in a terrible experience for what it was – a way for you to not have to choose for yourself?"

Silence again filled the airwaves between us.

"I would never have considered..."

"Zoe, your heart wants to be free, to explore again, to be carefree and bold. You'll have to let him go to reclaim that part of you. Are you willing?"

Within 15 minutes, the rapist's energy was long gone and in his place was the vibrancy of a young woman housed in a middle-aged woman's body. If I had been in the room with her, I would have bet she looked 18 again.

Following that release, Zoe returned to her carefree ways, lost 30 pounds and made pivotal decisions for her life and her business. During a phone conversation, she shared that the lightness and gusto for life she had as a young girl was her near-constant companion.

Returning to Trust & Love

"I've ruined my family's lives," he cried. Through deep inhales, a man I'll call Daniel poured his heart's suffering out. He was ashamed. He felt horrible about what he had done to his family. "I have lost everything. It's all gone. There's nothing I can do to fix it."

I knew Daniel was deeply loved by his family. They did not blame him for the situation he was in, but he continued to blame himself for years following his crisis. He ached from the despair he felt. He couldn't forgive himself for a situation where he felt he was completely to blame for what had happened. Had the issue come from some unforeseen problem – some external, unknown force – maybe he could have forgiven himself, but this was a situation he brought upon himself. He deeply wanted to find peace, but he could not quit blaming himself.

"The way I see it," I started. "You've got two choices. You can keep blaming yourself for the rest of time and stay stuck where you are, or you can forgive yourself and get back in the saddle and create something new. Your choice."

"You don't get it! I have RUINED my family's *lives!*" he wailed.

"I *do* get it. You *feel* like you've ruined your family's lives. I get that. But, what's the truth here? Is everyone alive? Does everyone have a roof over their head? Is everyone healthy? Is everyone eating three meals a day? Do you have a car to drive? Do they? So you lost some money. Don't you see you still have everything that is most important?"

"Yes, but I have RUINED our plans for the future! It's all gone! We had to move to a smaller house!"

"Plans change all the time. You don't know what's going to happen next. Your future plans may become even *better* because this happened to you! You only think you know what is happening right now. You don't know the future. You don't know what is possible – what could be even better *because* you've gone through this experience!"

I could feel how heavy his heart felt. It felt like it was weighed down by the Titanic. I felt for how badly he felt for being the reason his family had lost most of their money. I knew exactly how he felt. I had gone through a similar experience myself. I had also gone through the phase of understanding that those who stay with you after a crisis like that stay *by choice*. Many people lose their loved ones in a crisis like that, his entire family still loved him deeply.

"What I know is that if you keep blaming yourself, you won't create anything new. If you don't create anything new, there's not much of a chance for a future that looks different than what you have going on right now. Are you willing to try to let go of this? For your family's sake?"

Often, people want to punish themselves when they feel they have been 'bad' or done something 'bad.' Only when presented with a benefit for another person will they open themselves to letting go of their self-deprecating patterns. What he could not see was that in wanting to punish himself for being bad and not being good enough, he was hurting those he loved the most even *more*. He was robbing his family of his very presence, his love, his amazing heart and zeal for life. His daughters loved him dearly, so did his wife – ultimately, it was his love for *them* that took him to loving himself enough to forgive himself and let go of the shame that had shackled him for years.

Within two years, Daniel's desperate financial outlook completely reversed itself. Many miracles occurred one-by-one to show him that, yes, he could be trusted with money, yes, he could be responsible again, and yes, he was a good husband, father and provider. The more he trusted God and himself, the more everything turned around. The greater gift in forgiving himself was found in realizing that no matter how bleak a situation, he could find strength in trusting his infinite connection with God.

Letting Go of Limiting Connections to Others in Favor of Infiniteness

"No one understands what it is like to be overlooked repeatedly for a job promotion," a client I'll call Ian said with resignation in his voice.

He felt like a fire with an ember hanging on to the last log. The fire in his belly felt snuffed out.

"Why do you think they don't see you?"

He held on to the question for what seemed like a very long time. He finally said, "Well, I suppose because I am not willing to rub everyone's nose in how great I am like everyone else does."

The fire flared within him with each word. Anger can spark a flame when a person is falling down into apathy. His anger about the unfairness of his job situation shot off a flame.

"How much time each day do you spend watching others get what they want?"

"Oh, I see it all day long. Those people are running around bragging on themselves and acting like imbeciles!"

"Where are *you* when you are watching *them*?"

The question hung in the air. Ian said it aloud again to himself, "Where *am* I while I am watching *them*?"

"I guess I am just sitting there watching them take credit for everything. I sit there and boil when they do it. I am not like that. I can't do that. I can't make myself the center of attention to get a promotion!"

"Who says that's what it takes?" I asked.

"Well, it *must* be. Those are the people who are getting the promotions! I work twice as hard as they do! I am there in the morning before they get to work and I am the last to leave! I *deserve* a promotion – I do more work!"

"You believe more work equals promotion, but clearly it doesn't. You are focused on what others are doing, what others are getting. What are *you* creating?"

We worked with the Infinite Forgiveness Meditation to reset the energy between Ian and his boss, Ian and the co-workers he envied, and a couple of other people he shared the same energetic pattern with. He also forgave himself. Lighter after the energetic reset, he commented that "even if it didn't change anything at work, he at least felt better letting his bitterness go."

A week later, Ian called to let me know he was transferred to a new department in his company where he was now in charge of handling everything within that department. Yes, it was a department of one, but it was an *important* department within the company. It seems that the gentleman who had the position prior to this had been there for 12 years and had left the company the previous week to go to work for the competition.

What I found interesting is that this position was a perfect match for Ian – being the person in charge of *everything,* he was required to come in early, stay late and work many weekends. To *him,* this was what success looked like – his bitterness in his previous department grew from his inability to see success in a way that matched the success of those in his department. With the energetic ties cut and disconnected, he was free to find success that matched his own definition – all in the same company – and without him lifting a finger to try to find it!

Forgiveness in Business

"My daughter says you can help me."

The woman on the phone did not believe one word she had just uttered. I wondered why she had called at all.

"My daughter says you have helped her and you can help me."

"Well, I don't know. What is going on?"

"I have a man who rents a building from me and he is threatening to sue me!"

The unemotional woman's stoic energy turned into a tornado of fear.

"What can you do for me?" she demanded.

I avoided asking about any details. There was no reason to exacerbate her fear by going deeper into the story.

"Let's pray for him," I said.

"What? That's it? I knew you couldn't help me!"

"Let's work with a meditation to disconnect you from him so that *he* has a chance to do something different."

I shared several stories about how others had used this method to let go of conflicts with others. The woman begrudgingly agreed to try it. Within the meditation, I could see the man how angry he was with this woman. He wanted her to pay. He had threatened to sue her to make her feel what he was feeling – *powerless*. I could feel this woman had many patterns around making others feel small. In making others feel small, she could feel more powerful than she felt inside. Within herself, she felt powerless mostly. She felt sad for many other reasons, too. I felt bad for her. How sad she must feel each day.

When we completed the process, she said, "That's it? *That's* supposed to protect me from a lawsuit? I knew my daughter didn't know anything when she told me to call you!"

I hung up the phone knowing everything would be okay. The man did not feel like he had any real intention of suing.

My experience with this woman during our short phone call showed me she *could* drive someone to sue her, but this man – who he really was – didn't feel like he would do that.

Years later, in a chance conversation, I learned from this woman's daughter that the man never brought up the lawsuit again. He moved a year later without any conflict.

Forgiving a Parent Who Has Passed and Letting the Past Go Once and For All

Parents can have an immense hold on their child. I have worked with so many clients who have had most of their power held by a parent, and yet I have seen time and time again how great love can set them free.

A client I will call Rita called me because a friend of hers had referred her. I'll never forget this brave woman.

"I don't even know why I am calling you. My friend told me that you helped her and I just can't see how you are going to help me because I've done everything already – therapy for 10 years, belief clearing, spiritual retreats – I doubt there's anything you know that I haven't already done."

Her energy felt dense – like a big black cape made of thick wool surrounded her.

"Why did you call?"

"I guess because I still have hope – I haven't given up that somewhere there's an answer out there for me."

"What is it you would like help with now?"

"I don't really know."

"That might be part of the reason you haven't found an answer."

We laughed within the uncertainty of our conversation. The laughter found its way into our hearts.

"That's funny. So you are saying I haven't found an answer because I don't really want to find an answer."

"Actually, you are giving me way too much therapy cred

here," I said. "I mean that if you don't know what you want, how will you know when you have found it?"

"Ah, I see what you are saying."

I could feel her sweet soul underneath the big heavy black wool cape. Her heart and spirit felt like fizzy champagne – bubbly and kind. I felt intoxicated by it.

"I know exactly what I want," she announced after some thought.

"What's that?"

"I want to be rid of my dad."

"What do you mean?"

"I mean that I want to be done with thinking about my dad. He invades my mind – day and night. It's like I can't do anything without him peering over my shoulder. I know that must sound so weird and creepy."

"It's not weird at all. A lot of people feel that way."

"Really? They do? I didn't know that."

"Yes, it is a lot more common than you may realize. Many people walk around with their parents' voices in their heads telling them what to do all day long."

"Are you really ready to let your dad go?"

"Yes, of course. He died years ago. He was a brutally abusive man who beat my mom, me and my brother every chance he got. He was a horrifying nightmare to live with."

The way she shared this shocking story revealed how many layers were heaped on top of the emotion. She could have been saying, 'The sky is blue.' Her matter of fact demeanor shielded her painful memories. I shared with her how the Infinite Forgiveness Meditation works and how it can reach any energy anywhere and reset what was not love back into love. It could even work for those people who have passed away. Rita felt relieved.

"You mean I can let this go with a simple meditation? Honestly?"

"Yes, but you must remember that it is you that must not reach back for him once you complete the process. You wouldn't believe how many people let go of their burdens and then feel 'naked' and reach for them again."

"Oh, you can rest assured I will NOT do that!" she said.

During the meditation, I felt the cape fly off of her. Her bubbly spirit surged and filled up the room. Her energy had an exquisite quality that felt like it was straight from the heavens. Almost as if she was an angel.

I worked with Rita during two additional sessions where she learned why she reached for her father repeatedly in the days following our first session. She was absolutely positive if she could be free of her father and the memory of his brutal beatings, then she could finally be free to live her life. She knew for sure that she would *not* reach for these memories once they were released.

Little did she know that would not be the case. The next day, she found herself looking for those memories within the silence of her mind.

When she called the following week, she asked, "Why on earth would I go searching for those painful memories once they were gone? That makes absolutely no sense at all!"

"Healing – whether it is physical or emotional – affects people similarly. When they don't feel pain, they want to look for it. They want to make *sure* it is gone. When they go looking for what is gone, they end up reconnecting to the pain again, and then that stirs up the energy again. It's kind of like if you've had a pain in your leg and you wake up one morning and it's gone, you might keep looking for the pain. People do it all the time. Why, I have no idea, but they do."

"Well, I can't imagine any rational person who wants to revisit horrible memories."

"How long did you say you've been looking for an answer?"

"I didn't say specifically, but I would say it's been close to 20 years."

"In that time, would you say you were living your life?

Would you say that you were choosing what you wanted for your life?"

"No, I always felt like something was driving me to look for a way out."

"Is it possible you don't know who you are without your father? Without his energy hanging over you, who are you?"

She started to cry for the first time in our conversations. The grief overwhelmed her. "I don't know who I am without some reference to him. I am that girl with bruises on her legs she has to hide. I am the woman who can't get her shit together. I am the looney who can't seem to be helped by anyone. I am everyone's failure. Oh my God, I see it all so clearly now. Oh my God. It is so clear. It *isn't* him. It's not his fault. I chose to carry him with me all this time!"

I shared what I had seen during our first conversation – the black wool cape that enveloped her. His energy was like a cocoon that kept her light contained. I shared that her heart felt to me like bubbly, fizzy, sweet champagne.

"I *know* that girl. That *is* me! *That's* who I am! You see me! No one sees me!"

Rita's sweet energy felt like it floated up in little bubbles. I could feel her father's presence nearby. He celebrated with her, too.

Rita worked with this method over the following month to slough off layers and layers and layers of energy – some the direct result of her experiences with her abusive father, many more were from the many other people who had come into her life who were just like her father. She had been playing out this one pattern repeatedly for decades.

Today, Rita is a spirited artist who makes her living doing what she loves most – creating beauty. The girl with the heavy black wool cape is now free to live her life full of the bubbly joyful light she is.

16

INFINITE FORGIVENESS MEDITATION
QUICK CONNECTION - STEP-BY-STEP

Once you have worked with the Infinite Forgiveness
Meditation and understand how the method works for you,
a simple memory jogger may be all you need to quickly
connect. Here's the meditation step-by-step without
instruction.

*Please note: Working energetically with others is a privilege and
requires an understanding of how you may affect others during this
process. Please read the more in-depth explanation of working with
this meditation before proceeding. Thank you.*

1. Lie down. Relax your body.

2. Connect to intense feelings of love.

3. Expand the feeling of love inside your body and allow
    that sensation to expand so that it feels like the energy
    is slightly larger than your physical body is. Float in this
    energy and notice how you feel.

4. Allow the image of the person being forgiven to come

up in your mind's eye.

5. Notice how far apart you feel from this person.

6. Next, see a shell pink thread connecting you and the other person heart-to-heart.

7. Once connected to the other person, notice how you feel. If you do not feel well, ask to feel better. There is no need to suffer.

8. Send the feeling of love and joy to the other person. Think of this like you are sharing how you feel through this heart thread.

9. Listen/watch what happens next. Each time is different and perfect for you/the other person. The person will naturally move closer to you as you send love.

10. Once the person is nose-to-nose, complete forgiveness in a way that feels good to you.

11. Take a moment to feel what you are feeling. Thank God for the infinite support you've received.

12. When you are ready, begin to come back to your body and slowly rise from your reclined position.

17

A NOTE FROM TINA

Infinite Forgiveness is one of the most amazing tools I have experienced. It is my privilege to share it with you and to illustrate these ideas about how powerful each of us is. And to share how we energetically impact ourselves and others. I hope that by learning how powerful each thought, each emotion you have is, that you will consider how you impact yourself and others on a daily basis.

In this understanding, I hope you will use this tool to let go of the emotions that take you away from being the person you were born to be. By choosing to *be more* you can gift the world with your amazing presence. And, by *being more*, you can *have* more of everything you've ever dreamed of for yourself. Life *can* feel like a magic carpet ride...one where you feel lovingly supported in every way and free to live the life you've always dreamed of. It's a life worth believing is possible for you. Because it is. It starts today...moment to moment...choose to be and experience *more*.

While I believe in the healing power of prayer and the infinite power of grace, I do believe that sometimes we may also need help in the here and now.

In like manner, you would not rush to an acupuncturist to set a broken limb, spiritual practices have their time and place. You can always *combine* spiritual practices with help in the here and now. If you are in an abusive relationship, you may need help outside of this meditation – pray for guidance for what help to seek and reach out to those who can assist you. You can always use Infinite Forgiveness *with* outside help to alleviate or lessen the drama that may be associated with your current situation, but do also reach out for the help you may need. There are many people in the world who are ready and willing to help you. When you pray for guidance and ask for where to go for help, God will send you to exactly the right resource for you. Listen!

This advice also goes for those of you who may be depressed, who may be stuck or who may have real challenges within. Whether you choose to see a therapist, a doctor, a life coach or a spiritual advisor, listen to yourself and do what is best for you. Again, if it works for you, pray for where to turn.

One of the hardest things I've ever had to do and have had the honor of learning is to learn how to receive from others. We come into this world with others, we live our lives with others, and we are meant to be with others. We are never, ever alone. Believing you are alone is one of the greatest lies alive in this world. You may *feel* alone, but you can't truly be alone unless you choose to be alone. Accept the love that comes your way…dare to believe others *do* care.

Accept love from others. Accept and be the love that you are. Fill yourself up and then share the love you are with the world. The world is less when you aren't fully alive in it. Come share yourself with us!

You are special and worthy of living a life full of love and beauty. No matter what your life is like today, you can experience *more!*

ABOUT THE AUTHOR

Tina R. Ferguson, Ph.D. creates books and programs for people who know life is meant to be more – more fulfilling, more magical, more creative, more connected, more abundant. She offers you practical wisdom, actionable steps and a commitment to help you be authentically who you were born to be – in both life and in business. As a visionary catalyst, she brings a new perspective to everyday life and business challenges and ushers in fresh possibility that comes from a true change in perspective.

Those looking for "more" read her books, plug-in to her Queen of Dreams Radio, access her chock-full website, and attend her transformational workshops, and discover they *can* be living the life of their dreams in less time than they ever thought possible. In a matter of days, people who work with her breakthrough tools and practical principles begin to feel that living a truly authentic life full of purpose, passion, presence and profits is actually POSSIBLE. You can find many of these tools posted for free on her website at www.TinaFerguson.com.

She is an award-winning writer who has written virtually everything from poetry, essays, and short stories to books in the areas of energy management, spiritual inspiration, and business and marketing strategy. An accomplished business strategist and executive coach in her former career, Tina has been featured in *The Dallas Morning News*, *The Dallas Business Journal*, *Exclusively Dallas* and on the NBC5 evening and morning news in Dallas.

She is the author of *Must Be Present to Win: How to Get Out of the Ditch and Plug In To Your Passion* and way too many other things to list here.

WHAT CLIENTS SAY

"In the past three months of working with Tina both my personal energy and my business success have sky rocketed to new levels. I have done other similar type of work with coaches but never have my own understanding and vision come together so quickly and powerfully. I know what I need to do and am committed to doing it. Working with Tina is like taking the Concorde, the fast track to where you want to be. Get ready to enjoy the ride."

- Minette Riordan, Ph.D., www.MinetteRiordan.com

"Something clicked inside when I heard you speak. I think that something was me. All at once, it was apparent. What am I waiting on? This was the clarity I asked for. Thank you!"

-Workshop Participant Questionnaire, Identity Unknown

"My experience with the Hearts of Fire Retreat and Tina was transformational and miraculous! I rediscovered parts of myself I had hidden away for a long time. It was the kind of insight and movement that would take years to accomplish ordinarily. Tina delivers BIG! There are no words to describe such internal growth in such a short period. The information affected me on all levels and I would recommend this program to anyone who wants to grow/prosper/love bigger/live a fuller more stress-free life not live in pain anymore; and who wants to participate FULLY in life!"

- Dorine Fernandez, Founder, Triad Adventures
  www.TriadAdventures.org

"If you want to step up to the leader that you were born to be, to act on your inner voice, to grow your business and be the success you know you can be, work with Tina. She has been an amazing guide to me in aligning my business with my personal desires and talents. She knows how to get to the heart of the matter, assist you to overcome blocks and

move forward very quickly. Your investment will be returned many times over. Tina continues to hold me up to the vision we created together and offers ongoing support and resources that inspire me and keep me moving in inspired action."

-Kathy Garland, Transformational Leader
www.KathyGarland.com

"How does it feel to know you have completely changed the course of a life? How does it feel to hear you have completely changed the course of MANY lives? What greater gift is there than to show people where they are, show them who they REALLY are, and to give hope by assisting in reconnecting their true selves with their current being? Thank you does not seem to be enough, but, thank you."

-Susan Tate, Award-winning Designer & Entrepreneur

"From the moment I set the intention to work with Tina Ferguson this past summer, things began to move for me. In our first session together, I had some aha moments and began having breakthroughs which propelled my business forward very fast. I was able to make decisions that positively impacted my business, including revamping, re-partnering and relocating. My first week in her program, I quadrupled my business, and it has continued to grow steadily this year. Tina has helped me to grow both as an individual and as a business woman, and I am benefiting greatly from her guidance. Working with Tina this year, I have been able to fill in the missing pieces to doing work that I love and being successful and fulfilled. Tina will take you on the fast track if you are ready for it, and she will challenge you in great ways to create and live your best life."

-Michelle Barr, M.Ed., Success Coach, Speaker & Author
www.MichelleBarr.com

DISCOVER *MORE* AT

WWW.TINAFERGUSON.COM

*"I AM NOT WHAT HAPPENED TO ME,
I am what I choose to become."*

– CARL JUNG

"Choose to become more."

– TINA R. FERGUSON

People I Would Like to Forgive

What I Feel I Need Forgiveness For

What I Want to Resolve In My Life

Notes & Thoughts

Notes & Thoughts